WRITE IT

DOWN,

. . .

let it go

WRITE IT

DOWN,

. . .

let it go

a worry relief journal

LINDSAY KRAMER

CHRONICLE BOOKS
SAN FRANCISCO

ISBN 978-1-4521-4919-6

Manufactured in China

Design by Tonje Vetleseter
Text by Lindsay Kramer

10

Chronicle books and gifts are available at special quantity
discounts to corporations, professional associations, literacy
programs, and other organizations. For details and discount
information, please contact our corporate/premiums
department at corporatesales@chroniclebooks.com or at
1-800-759-0190.

Chronicle Books LLC
680 Second Street
San Francisco, California 94107
www.chroniclebooks.com

INTRODUCTION

FINDING CALM in our daily lives is an important way we reflect on and reconnect with our surroundings. Sure, we all face worries each day, from concerns about whether we locked the front door to anxieties about our financial future, but there are many ways we can learn to let go and create a sense of relaxation and peace.

Many cultures deal with life's obstacles using a range of practices from exercising, cooking, and traveling to spending time with loved ones. Eastern cultures have developed meditation and yoga as a means of stress relief, which are now both readily practiced across the globe. Russian and Mediterranean cultures literally blow off steam in *banyas*—saunas—as a way to relax while interacting with members of their community. Swedish workers enjoy *fikas*, or coffee breaks, to socialize, de-stress, and seek support during an otherwise busy workday. South American parents place tiny "worry dolls" under the pillows of their sleeping children to remove troubles from their dreams. Almost all forms of faith and religion promote prayer as a tool in stress response; even twelve-step recovery models rely heavily on the concept of giving up control within our everyday lives to a Higher Power.

The process of letting go of control is a practice within itself. Often, we try to control a troublesome situation as a way to resolve it. Instead of solving the problem, this creates a cycle of anxiety from the situation itself, concern over fixing the problem, and increased anxiety from the lack of a solution. As a psychotherapist, I regularly challenge my clients to surrender the uncontrollable and deal instead with what can be controlled, encouraging focus on a solution and not an unsolvable problem.

Talking through fears and problems within psychotherapy has widely been proven to reduce distress while resulting in mental, emotional, and physical improvements. Furthermore, many forms of therapy use writing as a tool for healing and self-soothing. Psychologist James W. Pennebaker took this method a step further in his work on the Basic Writing Paradigm, which maintains that writing about significant emotional experiences provides the same benefits as talking therapies. He found that the writing process allows for a reevaluation of negative emotions, which can significantly decrease anxiety levels. Better yet, writing for several consecutive days for fifteen to thirty minutes per session resulted in a decrease in intrusive thoughts, a reduction of heightened emotions, and an improvement in physical and immune functioning, to name a few. Put simply: Developing a writing practice can not only be cathartic and therapeutic, it has long-term benefits as well.

Expressive writing also offers unique benefits when compared to other methods of stress reduction. Beyond the immediate conveniences—writing is free, it can be done almost anywhere, and it doesn't require a twenty-four-hour cancellation notice—the physical act of writing enables you to visually process your concerns because you watch them being written down. Expressive writing also allows for full disclosure and complete authenticity without the often-feared judgment in sharing feelings with another. You as both the worrier and the writer are empowered to let out your fears, insecurities, and mistakes while simultaneously validating yourself for having the courage to release them. Writing both allows for and results in strength, honesty, and compassion as you are giving yourself complete permission to leave it all on the page without inhibition.

And that's where this journal comes in. This is your space to freely write out your troubles and to allow them to be contained only on the page. Whether you use this as a daily practice or whenever needed, treat every writing experience as an opportunity for processing and releasing.

Use the left-hand side of the pages to write down what's bothering you, while the right-hand side of the page is for practicing the act of letting go by means of problem-solving, reframing the challenge, or simply processing what you wrote on the other side.

To help you get in the mind-set of letting go, try this exercise.

VISUALIZATION EXERCISE

Imagine your stressful and worrisome thoughts spinning uncontrollably through your head. Now, visualize yourself lassoing those troublesome thoughts and feelings and pulling them down to the base of your skull and then out of your head completely.

Identify where the other vexing words are within your body and collect those as well. Search your chest, your stomach, your shoulders, your back, your legs, and your arms to find any remaining stragglers. Notice where this group is located within your body.

Now that the worries are all rounded up together, imagine that they are making their way through your chest to your arms, and through your arms down to your fingers. Then, from your fingertips, feel them trickle through your pencil or pen and breathe them out onto the page. Sit with your feelings and thoughts as you write and experience what it's like to see them on the paper as you let them go.

Now, decide that those worrisome and stressful words are imprisoned on the page, never to make their way back into your body. Allow them to be held captive on the paper because they have found a new home and a new space to fill. Praise yourself for having taken the time to write down these woes. You can return to this journal tomorrow to lasso in a new thought, or the next time you feel overwhelmed and are searching for relief. For now, welcome the resulting calm into your life instead.

"If you do not breathe
through writing, if you do
not cry out in writing,
or sing in writing, then
don't write."

—ANAÏS NIN

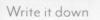

Write it down

"Nothing will
work unless
you do."

—MAYA ANGELOU

START THE SOOTHING PROCESS EVEN BEFORE YOU WRITE

Before you open the journal, employ a mindfulness strategy such as deep breathing or retreating to a quiet place. These techniques will allow a clearer mind and a sharper focus while you are channeling your thoughts and feelings onto the page.

"Remember, the
entrance door
to the sanctuary is
inside you."

—RUMI

"It's not stress that
kills us; it is our
reaction to it."

—HANS SELYE

Write it down

"Calm mind brings inner
strength and self-confidence,
so that's very important for
good health."

—HIS HOLINESS
THE 14th DALAI LAMA OF TIBET

CATCH IT, CHECK IT, CHANGE IT

While you're writing and processing, catch the anxious thought, check it to see whether it's detrimental to your thought process, and change the thought if it is. This trick of "catch it, check it, change it" can be repeated every time a troublesome idea is weighing you down and keeping you anxious.

"Inner peace begins the
moment you choose not
to allow another person
or event to control your
emotions."

—**PEMA CHÖDRÖN**

Write it down

"One way to boost our willpower and focus is to manage our distractions instead of letting them manage us."

—DANIEL G

VISUALIZE YOURSELF IN A CALM PLACE

*Whether it's your favorite location in
the world, sitting on the beach or gazing
up under the stars, visualize yourself in
a calming environment and assign positive
emotions and thoughts to that place.
Return there whenever you need to invite
calm into your life.*

"There is only one way
to happiness, and that is
to cease worrying about
things which are beyond
the power of our will."

—EPICTETUS

"You should sit in meditation
for twenty minutes a day,
unless you're too busy; then
you should sit for an hour."

—OLD ZEN SAYING

GIVE YOURSELF A "WORRY PERIOD"

Schedule a time each day where you are allowed to worry and write those thoughts out here. During the worry period, you're allowed to write out whatever is troubling your mind. Make the rest of your day a worry-free period. This will encourage you to use the journal as a container and to practice leaving it all on the page.

"I can shake off everything
as I write; my sorrows
disappear, my courage
is reborn."

—ANNE FRANK

"You can make
anything by writing."
—C. S. LEWIS

SOLVABLE OR UNSOLVABLE?

Distinguish between a worry that you can solve and something over which you have no control. If you can solve the worry, come up with strategies or solutions to deal with it. If not, it isn't your worry to deal with and you have the luxury of letting it go.

"If a problem is fixable, if a situation is such
that you can do something about it, then
there is no need to worry. If it's not fixable,
then there is no help in worrying."

—HIS HOLINESS THE 14th DALAI LAMA OF TIBET

"In the process of letting go
you will lose many things
from the past, but you will
find yourself."

—**DEEPAK CHOPRA**

WRITE
LISTS

On the left-hand side of these pages, write down three stressors, and on the right-hand side, identify three corresponding solutions. Be realistic about what you can do to manage them.

"If I do not write to
empty my mind,
I go mad."
—LORD BYRON

"Fill your paper
with the breathings
of your heart."
—**WILLIAM WORDSWORTH**

SCHEDULE
TIME AFTER
JOURNALING

*Just as you can schedule time to write,
designate time to relax afterward. Book
a massage, go for a walk, make food
for the ones you love. Reward yourself
for having processed your feelings.*

"Cry. Forgive. Learn. Move on. Let your tears water the seeds of your future happiness."

—STEVE MARABOLI

"Worrying is carrying tomorrow's load with today's strength, carrying two days at once. It is moving into tomorrow ahead of time. Worrying doesn't empty tomorrow of its sorrow, it empties today of its strength."

—CORRIE TEN BOOM

EARLY ON, EARLIER IN THE DAY IS BEST

It takes practice to be able to ensure that your worry period doesn't spill over once you are done writing. Try writing early in the morning so you can give yourself plenty of time during the day to practice "letting go" by bedtime.

"Start writing, no matter
what. The water does
not flow until the faucet
is turned on."

—LOUIS L'AMOUR

"Write while the
heat is in you."
—HENRY DAVID THOREAU

CREATE A STRENGTHS LIST

List three of your personal strengths you are thankful for. Write down how you are going to use them more often.

"Nothing can dim
the light that shines
from within."
—MAYA ANGELOU

CREATE A CALMING TOOLKIT

Think of a metaphorical toolkit that you can use to store your peace. Visualize yourself opening the kit when you need to invite calm into your life, and close it again when you feel more relaxed. Use as often as needed.

"Your intuition knows
what to write, so
get out of the way."

—RAY BRADBURY

"Throw up into your
typewriter every
morning. Clean up
every noon."
—**RAYMOND CHANDLER**

THERE'S ALWAYS ANOTHER WAY TO LOOK AT SOMETHING

Identify your fears and troubles and see if you can't look at them from another perspective. Don't let your fears overcome you, but instead identify what's really behind them and what you can do to overcome them instead.

"A word after a word
after a word is power."

—MARGARET ATWOOD

"Each one has to find his peace from within. And peace to be real must be unaffected by outside circumstances."

—**MAHATMA GANDHI**

ONE ANXIOUS THOUGHT AT A TIME

Keep your attention on one worrisome thought at a time so you don't lose focus. Once you have finished processing that thought, you are free to move on to the next one. Every time you observe yourself trying to skip ahead, however, bring your focus back to the task at hand.

"Worry is most often a prideful way of thinking that you have more control over life and its circumstances than you actually do."

—JUNE HUNT

"My bursting heart
must find vent
at my pen."
—ABIGAIL ADAMS

FIND YOUR TOOLS

Identify which people, places, and/or things will help to bring about peace within your life. Utilize these "tools" to help you de-stress, and store them in your calming toolkit for future use.

"Writing is the only
thing that when I do it,
I don't feel I should be
doing something else."

—GLORIA STEINEM

"When we direct our
thoughts properly, we can
control our emotions."

—W. CLEMENT STONE

CALM THE BODY TO CALM THE MIND

Worry can get stuck inside your body. Observe where you store stress in your body when you're focused on your worries, and practice calming those places individually in order to better ease the overall tension.

"Nothing can bring you
peace but yourself."

—RALPH WALDO EMERSON

"Worrying is like sitting in a rocking chair. It gives you something to do but it doesn't get you anywhere."

—OLD ENGLISH PROVERB

FACE THE
FEAR AND DO
IT ANYWAY

*Review the contents you have written on the
facing page and identify any fears you
have expressed. Reflect on what it would be
like to face these fears and make a plan to
overcome them through action.*

"There is nothing to writing.
All you do is sit down at
a typewriter and bleed."
—ERNEST HEMINGWAY

"Letting go gives us freedom,
and freedom is the only
condition for happiness."

—**THICH NHAT HANH**

USE POSITIVE
SELF-TALK

*Encourage yourself, don't discourage yourself!
Your own words are powerful and make all the
difference in your attitude. Catch when you use
negative self-talk, check the process of how
it happens, and change it to something that's
positive and strength-based instead.*

"In order to carry a positive action we
must develop here a positive vision."

—HIS HOLINESS THE 14th DALAI LAMA OF TIBET

BREATHE

*Collect all the negative energy with
one deep breath in, and visualize
pushing it all out while you exhale.
Repeat three more times and sit
contentedly with the resulting peace.*

"Writing is a way of
talking without
being interrupted."
—**JULES RENARD V**

"All the art of living lies in
a fine mingling of letting
go and holding on."
—**HENRY HAVELOCK ELLIS**

SET THE MOOD WITH MUSIC

Music is the perfect accompaniment to writing, so choose soothing music while you dive into your journaling.

"If you want to
conquer the anxiety of
life, live in the moment,
live in the breath."

—AMIT RAY

"Surrender to what is.
Let go of what was. Have
faith in what will be."

—**SONIA RICOTTI**

LOOK BACK
AND REFLECT

Look back at previous journal entries to reflect on what you have already written down and let go. Reviewing what you've expressed in the past can bring you clarity

"Some people believe holding on
and hanging in there are signs of
great strength. However, there
are times when it takes much
more strength to know when to
let go and then do it."

—ANN LANDERS

"Happiness depends
on ourselves."

—ARISTOTLE

MOVE A MUSCLE, CHANGE A THOUGHT

Focusing on your body allows for redirection of your thoughts and helps you to process stress without having to directly think about it. Try incorporating movement such as yoga, dancing, walking, or deep breathing.

"I write entirely to find out
what I'm thinking, what I'm
looking at, what I see and
what it means. What I want
and what I fear."

—JOAN DIDION

ACCEPTANCE
OVER
ANYTHING

*Sometimes it takes much more work to
change something than it does to accept it.
You can't always change everything, but
you can practice accepting it.*

"Acceptance doesn't mean
resignation; it means under-
standing that something is
what it is and that there's got
to be a way through it."

—MICHAEL J. FOX